MY CRAFTY BIZ

A Step-by-Step Guide to Building a Successful Arts & Crafts Business

by Tricia Ulberg

© Copyright 2021 Tricia Ulberg | Spicewood & Rose. All rights reserved.
www.spicewoodandrose.com

Cover and interior design by Tricia Ulberg.

Table of Contents

- INTRODUCTION 2
  - REASONS TO START A BUSINESS AROUND YOUR CRAFT 3
  - WRITE DOWN SOME GOALS 6
- **STEP 1: BUILD YOUR BRAND** **8**
  - CREATE A VISION BOARD 9
  - NAME YOUR BUSINESS 12
  - MAKE YOUR MARK: GET A LOGO DESIGNED 14
- **STEP 2: MAKE YOUR PRODUCTS** **17**
  - FIND SUPPLIERS AND MANUFACTURERS 18
  - QUALITY IS SUPER IMPORTANT 20
  - PACKAGING DESIGN 22
- **STEP 3: MONEY, TAXES, AND (BORING) LEGAL STUFF** **24**
  - LEGALLY FORM YOUR BUSINESS 25
  - HOW TO GET PAID 27
- **STEP 4: OPEN SHOP AND START SELLING, HOORAY!** **29**
  - PRICE YOUR PRODUCTS 30
  - VENDOR EVENTS: HOW TO MAKE THEM SUCCESSFUL 32
  - HOW TO SET UP AN AWESOME VENDOR BOOTH 36
  - LAYOUT IDEAS FOR CANOPY TENT BOOTH SPACES 38
  - FORM YOUR OWN VENDOR GROUP 42
  - WHOLESALING – HOW TO GET YOUR PRODUCTS IN RETAIL STORES 44
  - WAYS TO SELL ONLINE 47
- **STEP 5: MARKETING YOUR BIZ** **50**
  - SOCIAL MEDIA ADVERTISING 51
  - THE BANDWAGON 51
  - HOW TO GET ORGANIC FOLLOWERS 52
  - PAID ADVERTISING 53
  - INSTAGRAM—MY FAVORITE SOCIAL MEDIA PLATFORM FOR CRAFTY BIZ OWNERS 54
- **CONGRATS, YOU'RE A BUSINESS OWNER!** **65**
  - WRITE A BUSINESS PLAN 66
  - WHAT TO DO WHEN YOU GET STUCK 67
  - KEEP GOING, GIRL! 68

INTRODUCTION

Hello! I'm Tricia Ulberg, a graphic designer and crafty business owner living in Austin, Texas. I am a serial crafter — I've never met a craft that I haven't loved or wanted to try. I also love business and marketing, and I have an entrepreneurial heart.

I have been selling my arts and crafts for over twenty years, and I've learned a thing or two about what works and what doesn't. I've owned a brick-and-mortar paper crafting store, I've designed and launched my own rubber art stamp line, and I currently run a screen-printing biz. I know how to get handmade products out to the world and into the hands of those who appreciate them.

I also have a design and marketing background, and I've included plenty of tips to help you build a brand around your biz that will help you stand out from your competitors. This is so important!

I love small business owners and the creative spirit that is cultivated when we support each other. I wrote this book so that I can share what I've learned with you, my crafty soul-sisters, in the hopes that it will help you design and launch a business around your craft that is as wonderful as the products you are making.

Reasons to Start a Business Around Your Craft

The two things I hear most often from crafty girls when trying to decide whether or not to start a business:

"I want a job where I can feel creative and do what I love!"

Or conversely, "I am afraid that I'll ruin the love of my hobby by turning it into a job."

Ever heard the phrase, "Do what you love and you'll never work another day in your life"? I believe that you absolutely CAN do what you love and make an income at the same time. When you are happy with what you're creating, your enthusiasm will shine through. The right customers will love and appreciate what you do, you just need to find them!

If you are worried that trying to profit from your hobby will make it less enjoyable, try shifting your mindset. Earning an income with your arts and crafts, whether it be a side-hustle or a full-time job, can allow you to be your own boss, set your own hours, and spend your time working on creative projects that you care about. Stay true to your craft and don't change what you're creating based on what you think is selling better for other artists. Instead, focus on marketing techniques to find the right target audience for your product.

Find Your Why

What excites you about the idea of starting your own biz? Maybe you're earning money for a dream vacation, or you're helping a child with college tuition. Maybe you have big dreams for a super successful business that lets you quit your day job.

My best and most important tip regarding your Why is this: Whatever your reason for starting a biz around your craft, start from day one to treat it like a business. The most successful crafty biz owners I know have always done this. It's easy to spot someone who has decided to give it their all, and that energy is contagious. Pour your heart and soul into your biz and people will recognize your efforts. Go after your dreams, girl!

Create a Workspace That Inspires You

Our environment has a big impact on our creativity levels, so carve out a space that is just for you. Find a place where you can dedicate yourself to your work. Maybe it's an empty corner in your house, a spare room, the garage, or a workshop. Organize your space so you have easy access to the tools you need. Make it beautiful, so you feel creative and inspired every time you enter. This is where your amazing work begins.

My workspace is an extra bedroom that I turned into an art studio. I have screen printed posters on the walls that I've collected from different places, all my art supplies, screen printing supplies, and a big wood table. I painted the walls my favorite shade of green. It has a door that goes outside to the backyard, and I have a lawn chair on my deck where I can sit and take a break from whatever I am working on, enjoy my beautiful Texas hill country views and say hello to my favorite cactus growing in the yard. I love my "office!"

Write Down Some Goals

> *"The great danger for most of us lies not in setting our aim too high and falling short; but in setting our aim too low and achieving our mark."*
>
> -Michelangelo

Did you know that people who set goals, write them down, and check in on them often are more likely to be successful than those who do not?

I have a stack of pretty notebooks I collect in my office, and I'm constantly writing down my thoughts and ideas, as well as my long and short-term goals. I even have one in my nightstand drawer in case I get a 3:00 am idea (this happens all the time). It's usually a checklist of what I want to accomplish in the next week, or before a specific season. For example, my busy time is fall, so I'm really busy in the summer drafting my fall/Holiday season game plan. My notebooks keep me on track, and I enjoy crossing items off my to-do list. I always see progress in my biz with goal setting. And it's fun to look back at my notebooks and see the progress I've made.

Tip: Take notes about what you see working in your biz or what you'd like to change during your busy times so you can refer to them the following year. During the busy Holiday season, I always discover things about my current products that I would like to update and change, and I often have "light bulb moments" for new products based on what I find is selling best at the time. If I don't take notes, I don't always remember my ideas when planning time comes around. Sometimes our most creative ideas come during inconvenient times (like when we're busy at work, or my favorite— right before bedtime when I'm super tired) so be ready to write them down! You'll be glad you did.

Making Bread and Honey

Some of your goals should revolve around projected income. After all, this is why you're choosing to have a business!

Questions to ask yourself:

- How much will my start-up costs be?
- What will my profit margin look like after I've paid for all my supplies?
- How long will it take to reach my financial goals?
- What would I like my salary or hourly wage to be?

I sometimes see crafters avoiding this topic, because we are so happy to share our craft with people who appreciate our work that we are also happy to give it away for free. *But this is your business now, girl!* Time for a mind shift. Your craft and your time are valuable. You need to make enough money to keep moving forward in your business. Call it whatever you like— making bread and honey, bringing in the dough, baking cake. Make it your mantra. Because you are absolutely going to make money in your biz, and hopefully lots of it!

STEP 1: BUILD YOUR BRAND

"Brand is the promise, the big idea, the expectations that reside in each customer's mind about a product, service, or company. Branding is about making an emotional connection."

-Alina Wheeler

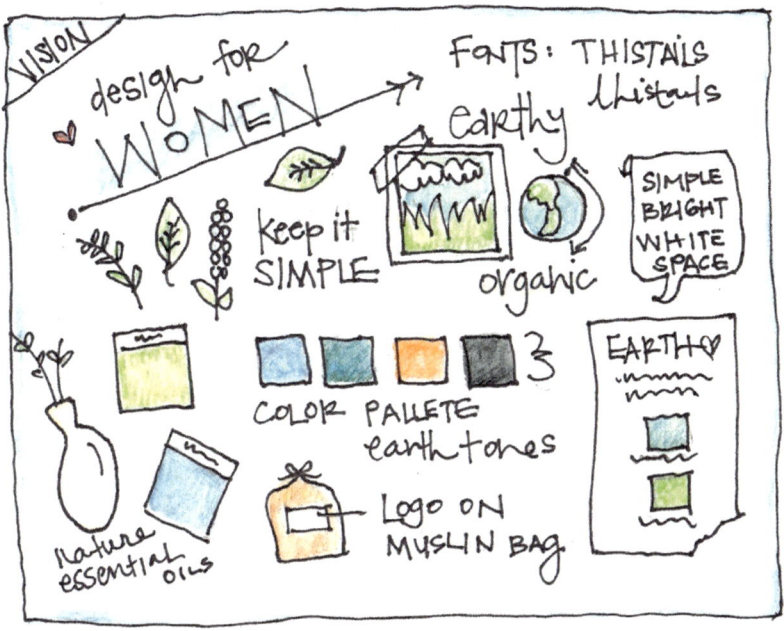

Create a Vision Board

What do you want your business to look like? I love creating vision boards. You can use a notebook, corkboard, or a blank wall in your workspace. Add color chips you like from the paint store, magazine clippings, favorite photographs of your work, and anything that inspires you. Start looking at how all these things relate to each other. Use it to help you visualize the look and feel of the company you are creating. If you ever get foggy on your message, you can refer back to it and do some course-correction.

Make a Brand Style Guide

Successful businesses put a lot of thought into making sure they are portraying the right image and sending the right message. Use your vision board to help you write a style guide for your biz that you can refer to when creating your marketing materials.

Things to include:

- Your logo and tagline
- Your color palette
- Your fonts/typography choices. Designers tip: choose one headline and one body copy font. Always use the same two fonts on all your packaging and marketing materials. Consistent typography use really helps establish your brand!
- Words to describe your look and feel. For example: soft, bright, classy, modern, simple, bold, fun, etc.

Here is an example of a simple style guide I have created for my business.

SPICEWOOD & ROSE *Style Guide*

FONTS: *Thistails* & THISTAILS SANS

BODY COPY: Avenir

COLOR PALETTE:

LOOK & FEEL: SIMPLE, CLEAN, BRIGHT

A few words about creating graphics for your biz. I use the apps in the Adobe Creative Cloud to design all my graphics and marketing materials. If you are interested in creating professional graphics for your business, start by learning Photoshop. This is also my favorite program for editing product photos and creating images to use on social media.

However, if you are not a designer, I highly recommend using an online graphics tool called Canva. Canva has templates you can start with for any type of graphic you are creating (social media ad, flyer, poster) and is very easy to use. You can create basic graphics for free or they offer a paid version that unlocks more features. Remember to refer to your style guide as you design your biz graphics and marketing materials to keep them on-brand.

Name Your Business

When naming your biz, choose carefully, because it's going to be attached to everything you do from here on out. Make a list of possible names and run them by your friends and family. Getting some outside perspective might be helpful. Sometimes we get tied to a name that really isn't right for us, and it takes someone else to point it out. You don't want to have to change it later, so make sure you feel completely confident in your choice.

Claim Your Domain Name

If you think you may want a website now or down the road, it's a really good idea to purchase a domain name as soon as you can. Your domain name is the URL people will type into a browser to connect to your website. The easiest and best thing to do is register your domain with your web hosting provider, but if you don't have a hosting account yet, don't worry about it. The most important thing is to claim your domain name while the one you want is available, and you can transfer it to your web host later.

A word of advice: once your business is "live" and public, there are people who may try to register your domain name before you do with the hopes of charging you more for it. I always recommend claiming your domain early in the formation of your business so you can avoid this happening to you, it can be frustrating!

Having a domain will also make it easy to create a custom business email address. You will look more professional when you have a unique email address opposed to Gmail or Hotmail. For example, "hello@yourcompanyhere.com" looks more professional than "yourcompany@gmail.com."

If you ever decide to set up an email newsletter campaign you will need a dedicated email address with your domain name. Most email marketing programs, such as Mailchimp, will recommend this so that your emails don't end up in spam or junk mail folders.

Make Your Mark: Get a Logo Designed

I am a graphic designer, so I have strong opinions about logos. Every business needs a logo, including yours, crafty girl! It doesn't matter the size of your biz—you need one. A logo is your mark, and it's just as important as the name of your biz. You will need one if you are on social media, for your business card, signage, product packaging, and advertising. If you are not an artist, consider hiring a graphic designer to help you create one. This is one thing that is worth investing in, you'll be glad you did it.

Make sure you have both a hi-res and lo-res (res is short for resolution) version of your logo image. Here's what this means:

- **Hi-res images are at least 200-300 dpi (dots per inch) and used for printed materials**, such as your business card, product packaging, or signage. If you try to print a lo-res logo, it will look blurry.
- **Lo-res images are 72 dpi and for use online**, such as social media or your website. File formats for lo-res images are usually .jpg, .gif, and .png files.

If you decide to hire a professional graphic designer, they will give you scalable artwork in several formats for both print and online use. To find a designer, try asking other business owners who they work with. I highly recommend trying to work with a designer that has been recommended to you before looking for one on freelance or logo creation websites.

Tip: A lot of social media apps and websites ask you to upload square shaped profile picts or shop icons. It's a good idea to have a logo that will fit well inside a square, or you can have two different versions of your logo. I pulled an element (the cactus) from my primary logo to create a square store icon.

Order Business Cards

Every biz owner should have business cards. You will get asked for yours. Order your biz cards as soon as you have your company name and logo designed.

Think about what information should be on there and who you will be giving it to. I have two different cards — a simple card with my website URL that I include with orders and hand out at my vendor shows, and a more detailed card with all my personal contact information that I share with store owners and wholesale customers. If you are on social media, it's a great idea to include your social media URL on your card so people can find and follow you.

There are lots of inexpensive ways to get your biz cards made — do a Google search and you'll see a few options. If you're working with a graphic designer, ask them to create a business card design with your logo that you can send to printers.

STEP 2: MAKE YOUR PRODUCTS

Time to get crafty.

Find Suppliers and Manufacturers

You may already know exactly how to make your products and where to buy your supplies. Of course, you will want to purchase supplies at wholesale prices if possible so it's easier to turn a profit.

One of the biggest roadblocks that I've seen holding back entrepreneurs is that they have an awesome product idea, but no idea how to get it made. If you are stuck, here's a success story to inspire you!

When I owned my paper crafting store, I was purchasing small batch artisan stamps from a local company. I loved them. As a designer and illustrator, I wondered how I could create my own line of rubber stamps. The problem is I had no idea how to get them made.

Fast forward a few years later. I closed my store and decided I wanted to design my own line of rubber stamps and wholesale them, just like the stamp company I used to purchase from. I convinced a good illustrator friend of mine to jump on board, and we started our company.

The first thing we did was look online for someone to manufacture our stamps. We found a company that made a lot of office supply rubber stamps, but it wasn't the best option because we were hoping for a company that specialized in art stamps. This was hard to find at the time. We even looked into purchasing our own rubber stamp making equipment — which would have been a heavy investment. We didn't really feel like learning how to make the stamps. We just wanted to design the artwork.

We had the idea to attend a large craft tradeshow called CHA to get ideas and see if we could find a manufacturer for our products. Long story short, it worked! There was a company at the show who offered exactly what we needed. The next year, we exhibited our company at the same show. We had a line of store owners waiting to talk to us before the doors even opened. It was brilliant!

Moral of this story — if you have a product idea but you're not sure how to get it made, don't let that discourage you. Keep researching online and calling and emailing until you get some leads. Going to tradeshows is an excellent idea — many product manufacturers attend these shows with the expectation that there will be people like you there looking for their services.

Quality is Super Important

A second story I have to share with you that I learned from running my rubber art stamp company is a lesson about the importance of creating a quality product.

When we were researching how to get our product made, we were lucky to find a great manufacturer who was using a high-quality rubber and made a beautiful stamp image. However, there was another product we were using on the back of our stamps to make them stick to a clear block that was a little less awesome. We didn't really know of a better solution, so we figured it was okay, and our designs would sell our stamps regardless. We just went with it, but to be honest, we knew it was a problem.

About six months later, a new cling mount product came on the market that a lot of other stamp companies started to use. We were a new business and had just invested a lot of our own money into getting our first round of stamp sets made. We didn't want to have to start over and throw out all the product we had just paid for! We thought about this decision long and hard. We knew that we needed to keep up with the competition, and we also knew that it was a better product. We came to the conclusion that we needed to start over, and we remade our entire line using the better-quality cling mount.

It was the best decision we could have made. Our sales increased, and we started getting reorders from a few stores who were already carrying our products and knew we had made the switch. I am not sure how long we would have lasted had we not made this change.

Lesson learned from this experience—when you are designing your product, always allow yourself room to tweak it when necessary, even if it means starting over. Making a quality product is super important, and people will always compare your products with others they see your competitors making. Don't give anyone any reason to doubt the quality of your product.

If you have a great idea, coupled with an excellent manufacturing technique, and you are only using the best materials available to create the best possible product, you are sure to hit it out of the park!

Packaging Design

How you present your products is just as important as the product itself. Attractive packaging will sell your product! Things to consider:

What types of packaging materials will work well with my product? For example, I make organic goat's milk and essential oil soap. I decided to package my soap in a burlap bag with my logo hand stamped on the front. It looks natural and matches organic qualities of my product.

What is the cost? You'll need to factor in the cost of your packaging solution when you price your products. You don't want your packaging to increase the cost of your product so much that it makes it hard to sell. On the other hand, beautiful packaging may give additional value to your product allowing you to charge more.

Who is buying my product? Is it for men, women, or both? Is it for children or adults? Is it geared toward people who are environmentally conscious? A product's packaging should appeal to your target audience.

Does my product need any required marks or text? Depending on your product and industry, you may be required to include a barcode, nutrition information, ingredients, etc.

How are people buying my product? Will it be sold primarily online, at a vendor event, or in a retail shop? For example, if you're selling online you may be mostly concerned with how easily the item can be shipped, and how it will be protected during shipping. If you're selling wholesale, you'll need to think about how your product will be displayed in retail stores (see wholesale section). This may also determine how you get your packaging made. If you are primarily selling at online and handmade artisan vendor events, it's completely expected for your packaging to look handmade as well. If you're hoping to get your product into retail stores, you may need to invest in some professionally designed and printed packaging materials.

How will I brand my product? This is an advertising opportunity! Make sure you are branding your packaging with your company name and logo. It's also completely appropriate to include your website URL somewhere on your packaging.

STEP 3: MONEY, TAXES, AND (BORING) LEGAL STUFF

Most creatives don't love managing the legal and financial side of running a business (I sure don't!) but it's crucial to your success. Get it out of the way so you can focus on the fun part, which is making and selling your products.

There are a lot of resources online that can help you walk through your options in terms of legally starting your business. Visit your Secretary of State's website and look for business start-up information.

Legally Form Your Business

First, you need to select a business entity. For many small artisans and crafters, a sole proprietorship is the simple choice. You don't need to file legal forms or pay any fees to launch a sole proprietorship. If you want to operate your sole proprietorship under a name other than your own, you'll need to file a certificate for a DBA (doing business as) name.

Depending on what you sell and where you're selling it from, you may also need to obtain certain business licenses — check your state or city requirements (it's always important to look up and comply with your local laws to avoid violations and fines). As a sole proprietor, you are personally liable for debts and obligations.

If your biz is rockin' and rollin' and you're so busy filling orders that you're going to quit your day job, it might be time to look into forming an LLC, or Limited Liability Company, to reduce your personal exposure to liability. Forming an LLC or incorporating your biz requires you filing specific forms as well as paying certain fees.

Seller's and Sales Tax Permits

A seller's permit, sometimes called a sales tax permit, is required if you are selling taxable products retail. You will need to register for a sales tax permit in your home state. You can find out what the current local sales tax rate is by visiting your state's comptroller's website. A quick Google search will also bring up this information. If you are collecting sales tax at a vendor show in a state other than where you hold a seller's permit, you may need to register for a temporary sales tax permit for the duration of the event. Every state has different rules! A great website to look up sales tax rules for your specific state is **www.taxjar.com**.

Tax ID Numbers

The Tax ID Number, also known as the Employer Identification Number (EIN), of your business will come in handy at numerous times throughout ownership of your company, such as when opening a business bank account or filling out a resale certificate. You should apply for your Tax ID Number as soon as you get your DBA name or business license. The only place to obtain your Tax ID Number is through the IRS. You can apply online at **www.IRS.gov**.

Resale Certificates

A resale certificate is required to buy your craft materials wholesale and sell retail. You do not need to pay sales tax on wholesale purchases. Most wholesale stores and suppliers will send you a resale certificate form before allowing you to purchase from them. You will need to include your Tax ID number on the form. If a form hasn't been provided to you, you can find a form through your state's comptroller's website.

How to Get Paid

There are lots of simple options for taking payments these days. I use Square, which comes with an online POS and inventory management system that is perfect for my products. You can order credit card readers that will work with your smart phone or tablet. And you have the option to send your customer a receipt. Having a Square account is free but there are transaction fees for processing credit card payments. Visit **www.squareup.com** for more information.

I also have an Etsy store, and for a fee they will handle all your payment processing. If you want your own ecommerce website to sell online, some good platforms are Shopify, BigCommerce, Wix, Squarespace, Etsy Pattern, among others — all of which will process payments.

A lot of customers are asking if they can pay via Venmo or PayPal these days. I will accept this payment method if they would prefer to pay this way instead of using a credit card. If a customer doesn't have cash or a credit card with them, this can be a life saver in terms of not losing a sale. I recommend having your business bank account linked to your Venmo or PayPal account so that you can keep your biz income separate from your personal income. There isn't an easy way to calculate tax, so be prepared to do this on your own, or include tax in the price of your product and round up to the nearest dollar. A lot of vendors do this anyways to make things easier.

Tip: If you are using PayPal or Venmo, make sure to open a business account so you can keep your sales separate from your personal income. It also feels more professional on the customer-side.

Invoicing

A big part of my biz is wholesale, and I like using PayPal's invoicing system for this. I can easily create an invoice via PayPal and my customers can pay me online.

A lot of stores ask for Net 30 terms, in which they will send you payment within 30 days of your invoice. For Net 30 orders, I have a PDF invoicing form that I found by doing a search online that I fill out and email.

If you are doing a lot of wholesale, it might be time to look into accounting software, such as QuickBooks, that can track your invoices and inventory.

It's a really good idea to have a business bank account so you can deposit checks that are made out to your business name. This will also be helpful when paying taxes. Look for banks that have low transaction fees and cater to small business. It's also a great idea to get checks printed with your business name.

STEP 4: OPEN SHOP AND START SELLING, HOORAY!

You have your product made, your business branding designed, and the legal stuff taken care of. It's time to get your products out into the world!

Price Your Products

Star, circle, and highlight this next line, and then write it down and stick it to your vision board, because it's super important:

Don't undervalue or underprice your products!

This is by far the biggest mistake I see crafters make. If you aren't making enough money to make your biz worth your time, you will lose interest, and it won't be fun anymore. And you'll quit. I have seen so many amazing crafters with amazing products quit for this very reason, and the world is missing out!

But you're thinking—everyone likes a deal, right? Not necessarily. When I first started wholesaling my flour sack tea towels, a boutique store owner told me I should be charging more. She explained that people wouldn't bat an eye if I increased the price by a few dollars. She was right. I am so glad I got this advice because I couldn't have continued to wholesale at the original price I had set. I realized that the boutique had a different kind of customer they were targeting than, well, Target!

The key is to price your products as high as you think someone will pay for a quality, handmade product. Don't price for what someone could purchase them at a big-box store like Target—this is not your target audience! The right people will understand and appreciate a handmade item verses one that is mass-produced.

Vendor Events: How to Make Them Successful

I love vendor events, sometimes called pop-up shops. I've had some very profitable events and some complete duds.

The best tip I can give you is to choose wisely. Not all vendor events are going to be worth your time! Do your research and ask yourself the following questions:

Who is the target audience for this event, and is it my target audience? For example, if it's an elementary school fundraiser, you know you'll get lots of Moms with young children attending. If you have a product that appeals to that demographic, go for it! Maybe it's an event at a local restaurant or winery — your audience is going to be a male/female mix and they may be stopping by your table before or after eating. Is it likely they will be interested in what you're selling?

What is the fee for vending? Do you see yourself easily making it up with your sales? What are they using the fee for — advertising or securing a good location? Be careful with vendor fees. You don't want to pay so much for your booth that the likelihood of making a profit is low.

What kind of setup will be required? Can you make do with a simple table display, or will you need to invest money into a tent, fixtures, signage, or other display pieces you don't currently have? If you are planning on doing a lot of vendor events, it might be worth investing in a good booth display.

How much advertising is being done for the event? If it's a good event, they should be doing plenty of advertising. Make sure you are advertising to your local customer base as well.

What does your competition look like? Is it a juried vendor event? How many vendors will be there that make products similar to yours? Be careful about participating in events that aren't picky about choosing quality vendors. This will have an impact on who attends. More people attend events that are known for having a great and varied selection of vendors.

Once you commit to an event, make sure you understand where you will be setting up your booth. I once participated in an event that assigned me a booth space right next to one of my competitors! It made us both very uncomfortable, and it made our customers uneasy too. You don't want to be competing with the person sitting right next to you!

The best events I have participated in have been juried shows with reasonable vendor fees that go primarily toward advertising. Free events can be just as good as events with vendor fees, and sometimes smaller events are better than big events depending on who attends.

One of my very best vendor events to date was a Holiday home party that a real estate agent friend threw for her clients. I sold everything I had with me!

There is a popular vendor show called Vintage Market Days that I participate in on a regular basis that is always a home run. They have events year-round and in many locations. It's a juried show, which means they are very selective in who they invite and the products that will be sold, which makes for a better show as you have less competition. If you're interested in juried shows, you may need to get on a waiting list. Keep trying! Once you've been accepted it's easier to participate in future shows.

As you participate in vendor events, you will learn which venues are right for you and your product.

Pop-Up Events

A lot of brick-and-mortar retailers like to host pop-up events, especially around a new product release or a holiday. Stores like to support local artisans, and it brings in new customers. I've had pop-ups at small boutiques and bigger retailers such as Nordstrom and West Elm. Follow these stores on social media to see if they host pop-ups, and then send them an email. You never know until you ask!

If you are wholesaling and there's a store carrying your products, this is a great opportunity for a pop-up. Ask if you can be on-site to interact with customers. People love meeting the artisan behind the products they are purchasing, and shop owners love it too because it helps boost sales. This is your chance to feel like a star!

Farmer's Markets

A lot of farmer's markets like to have a few handmade arts and crafts vendors set up alongside the regular food and produce vendors to add some variety to the market, especially around the Holiday season. I love farmer's markets because I know they attract customers who are interested in locally grown food and produce, so they are more likely to appreciate a locally handmade product too.

How to Set Up an Awesome Vendor Booth

You don't have to spend a lot of money on your table or booth – simple is always better! The goal is to make it easy for people to see your product. Style your booth like the pros by using the "triangle principle." Visualize a triangle as you arrange your products and use props to help you achieve this.

My best vendor display tip—do not have all your products flat on the table! People can easily miss your products when everything is flat. Sometimes they walk right by and don't even stop if they can't see what you're selling. Try using crates, wooden blocks, baskets, or other items to create height. Good signage is really important. It helps you advertise your biz—so take advantage of this opportunity! Make sure your signage is big enough to be seen by anyone who walks by your booth.

Also, have smaller signs out for any product that may need explanation (for example, the ingredients in your homemade soaps or bath bombs). If you get busy with customers, it will make it easier on you and the customer to have that information displayed.

Important—make sure to have all your products priced or display a price list. People do not like having to ask what the price of an item is, so make it easy for them.

Don't Forget the Shopping Bags

I can't tell you how many times I've forgotten to bring shopping bags with me—and people really need them at vendor events because they will be walking around and shopping at other booths, so they need a way to carry their purchases.

This is also a great advertising opportunity! Get a stamp of your business name and logo created and stamp your shopping bags. As your customers walk around the event with your bag in hand, they will be advertising for you.

Extra Little Somethings

Vendor events are a great way to grow your tribe. Display your biz cards at your checkout table and include one with every purchase. If you are on social media, you might ask people to follow you by including your social media name on your biz card or display a "follow me" sign. If you have an online store, you might consider including a coupon to shop online. Or throw a little trinket in your customer's shopping bag to remember you by, such as a piece of candy, sticker, etc.

Tip: I purchased a button maker and I design and make fun pinback buttons that match my designs to throw in a shopping bag. The customers love them. It feels like they are getting something free, and my cost is around 10 cents. Inexpensive advertising!

Payment Options

Plan on having a way to take both cash and credit cards. It's easy to accept credit cards these days with portable card readers (see How to Get Paid section). Occasionally I will see a vendor who only accepts cash and directs people to an onsite ATM machine. These vendors have a good chance of losing the sale—I don't advise doing this! You will have to pay a small fee for accepting credit cards, but it's better than losing a sale. You may want to adjust your prices if you think you'll be accepting a lot of credit card purchases.

If you are required to file sales tax, it's also helpful to run all your purchases (including cash sales) through the POS (point of sale app) that is connected to your card reader so it can manage the sales tax requirement for you. I use the Square POS app and it's easy to find how much tax I have collected when it's time to pay Uncle Sam.

Layout Ideas for Canopy Tent Booth Spaces

When planning your booth layout, your goal is to make sure your customers feel relaxed, engaged and ready to shop! If you're in a tent, think about how to maximize the space and make your products easy to see. Create visually interesting displays that move people around your space.

Don't make people walk all the way inside your booth to see what you sell. Some people will walk right by and not stop at all if they don't get a clear sense of what your business is without having to come inside. You need "curb appeal" to get them to walk in your front door. I like to display a sign near the entrance with a sample of my products. The idea is to grab their attention and entice them to enter my space.

Pretend you're a customer and walk around your space before the event starts. Are your best products front-and-center? How is the lighting? Do you easily see the checkout area? Is it fun? Is there enough color? Is your eye being drawn into your "triangle" displays? Give yourself some time to tweak your booth before show time—it can make a big difference!

SPICEWOOD & Rose
VENDOR BOOTH LAYOUT

T-SHIRTS IN HANGING CANVAS ORGANIZERS.
ONE DISPLAY BOARD WITH T-SHIRT DESIGNS.

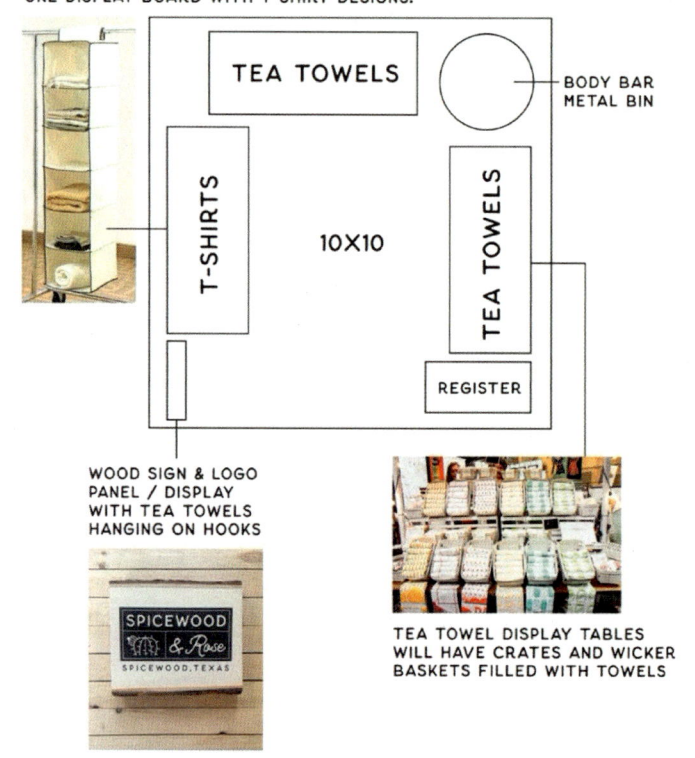

TEA TOWELS

BODY BAR METAL BIN

T-SHIRTS

10X10

TEA TOWELS

REGISTER

WOOD SIGN & LOGO PANEL / DISPLAY WITH TEA TOWELS HANGING ON HOOKS

TEA TOWEL DISPLAY TABLES WILL HAVE CRATES AND WICKER BASKETS FILLED WITH TOWELS

This is a layout example of my 10x10 booth space. I use it to help me visualize where I'll be displaying products, if I have any empty space to fill, and if there are any display fixtures I need to purchase before the event. I also like knowing exactly how I'll set up once I arrive, it saves time.

If you have a tent-sized booth but you don't have a lot of products, push your display tables toward the front of your space. There is no reason to make people walk all the way inside a half-empty tent.

Invest in a Good Quality Canopy Tent

I add this tip based on a lot of personal experience. If you plan on doing outside vendor shows and a canopy tent is required, invest in a good one! Research and read tent reviews. Also remember that a lot of shows have canvas color requirements. You're usually safe going with white.

I once set up shop at a three-day, outdoor vendor event that required that we bring our own tent. At the time, all I had was an okay-quality tent that I had purchased for under $100 on Amazon. I had weights for the tent legs which helped keep it secure (you'll need weights). But the problem at this particular outdoor event was that it was very windy, and the weights were not doing the job. I was going to be spending the entire event just trying to keep my tent from flying away if I didn't come up with a solution, fast! I did a desperate dash to Home Depot to see what I could come up with an hour before the event was supposed to start, and I ended up buying four big buckets and filling them with sand. I put a sand bucket next to each tent leg and secured it with rope. It helped a lot, and I survived. But my tent was still wobbly, and I was worried the entire time that it was going to break in half. It was really stressful!

After the event, I did some research and made an investment into a much nicer tent with thicker poles. Completely worth it. I also recommend getting tent walls so if it's sunny or rainy you can shield yourself and your products, this has saved me from other bad weather scenarios. That's the tricky thing about outside events, you never know what you're going to be dealing with in terms of weather. As the Boy Scouts say, be prepared!

Form Your Own Vendor Group

I'm about to share one of my very best vendor ideas with you. Consider forming your own vendor group and book your own events! It's a great idea because you have control over who joins your group and who your competition is. And you'll always get a spot in the event because you're in charge! I have done this myself, and it's been a great success.
In my vendor group, we limit the number of vendors selling similar products, and we only allow products that fit in well with the entire group. We are all responsible for finding and booking at least one event a year. I have found that asking HOAs, neighborhood community centers, or small businesses to host events for my group are a great place to start. A lot of them already have shopping events planned around the holidays, and by having your vendor group come, it saves them the headache of having to find individual vendors. All they have to do is coordinate with one contact person in our group and we do the rest!

We always offer to bring appetizers or door prizes, and most venues have been happy to let us set up without a vendor fee. We also help to advertise the event, and this can really appeal to small business owners who are looking for new customers. It's a win-win!

Here are some helpful tips regarding vendor groups:

Brand your group with a name and a logo. We have our logo on an A-frame board that we put outside our venues, and we always use our name and logo when we advertise our events.

Start asking your crafty friends if they would like to join your group. I've also recruited some great artisans that I've met while at other vendor events! If you're using social media, you could post a call for vendor applications.

Decide how many vendors to accept into your group, keeping in mind that most small businesses can only accommodate 15 or so vendors in their space, so smaller groups may be better. Also, establish some rules and guidelines. For example, everyone in my group must locate and book at least one event a year to participate.

Try creating a vendor GroupMe or Facebook Group. You will need an easy way to communicate and coordinate events.

Create a list of vendor names and their products to present to potential hosts. Give them the option to pick and choose the vendors they would like to invite.

Wholesaling – How to Get Your Products into Retail Stores

If you have the ability to price your products for wholesale, this can be a great way to grow your business. Wholesale orders can be more profitable than retail orders because of volume. You will most likely make more money selling 100 items wholesale than you will selling 10 items retail.

To sell wholesale, you must sell your product for 50 percent of the retail price. For example, if you are selling an item for $20, the wholesale cost will be $10.

Note: If you are selling both retail and wholesale, don't ever set your retail price less than what the stores can sell them for. They will notice, and they won't be happy about it. Your retail price should match or be more than the price your retail stores are setting.

Keep these things in mind if you want your product to be sold in retail stores:

Make sure you have good packaging and proper tags. Consider how a store might display your product—does it need a hook, will it be on a bookshelf, does it need a plastic sleeve, etc.

Create a well-designed flyer or catalog. Make it easy for stores to order. Having a website with a wholesale login is also a great idea.

Leave a product sample at the store. Something you should expect is that store owners will be too busy to talk with you when you drop by. And they are constantly being approached by vendors, so be respectful of their time. The best thing to do is leave a sample at the store with your catalog or flyer, and then follow up via email. Ask if you can make an appointment to stop by again when they have an opening in their schedule if they are interested in meeting with you.

Consider hiring a sales representative for your company. Some store owners will only work with sales reps because it's a real time saver for them to have one contact for several product lines and companies. If you aren't sure to how to find a sales rep, ask a store you work with if they have a recommendation (this is how I found my rep). Keep in mind that you will need to pay commission, so only consider this option if you have a big enough profit margin.

Once you have your product in a store, check back frequently to make sure there are no issues with how they are being displayed or sold. Ask the store owner what is selling and what is not. This will be great feedback for your next product line!

Remember that stores tend to order products a season or two ahead. Launch your Holiday and Christmas products in the summer, or even the spring. Spring products should be launched at the beginning of the year, summer products in spring, etc.

Tip: A lot of stores that carry my products have found me via my Etsy store, website, and social media accounts. Make sure to mention that you wholesale somewhere in your social media profile or on your website.

Wholesale Trade Shows

A really great way to get your product in front of retail store owners is by having a booth at a wholesale trade show. Retailers come from all over the country (sometimes the world!) to find new product lines to carry in their stores. I've participated in a few craft & hobby related wholesale shows with my rubber art stamp company, and it really launched our wholesale biz.

It can be very expensive to exhibit, however. Expect that renting your booth space will cost you in the thousands of dollars, and you will need to have a dynamic booth display.

Only consider this option if you have your product fully branded and your production method solid. You will be taking orders from retailers at the show and filling them when you return. Be ready to fill a lot of orders! This can be really awesome or really stressful depending on your production process and how much inventory you have ready to ship!

Ways to Sell Online

If you want to sell online, you have a few options. You can sell your products on an ecommerce website such as Etsy or Amazon Handmade, or you can create your own ecommerce website. There are pros and cons to both.

Selling on Etsy and Amazon is great because it comes with a built-in customer base and advertising. People specifically go to these sites to find handmade arts and crafts. However, you're limited to the platform in terms of branding and you will pay transaction fees for listing and selling your products.

Having your own ecommerce website gives you more control over the look and feel, and you can build a website around your brand. It's easy to add additional features such as an email newsletter signup, wholesale login, etc. A lot of people use Shopify, BigCommerce, Magento, or Wix, which offer easy-to-customize website templates. You will be charged a flat fee for website hosting.

Etsy Pattern is a blend between using Etsy and having your own website. For a flat monthly fee, you can create a website utilizing your existing Etsy listings. You can add additional items that you don't have listed on Etsy, set up an email newsletter campaign, blog, and use your own domain name. The checkout process and orders are managed through your Etsy account.

You may find that it's worth having both an Etsy shop and a stand-alone website depending on where your customers are coming from.

If you are new to selling online, I would recommend starting with Etsy or Amazon Handmade to help you grow your customer base. As your company gets bigger and you add more products, it may be less expensive to pay a flat monthly hosting fee for a website than Etsy/Amazon transaction fees.

Filling Online Orders

It's really important to make a good impression when you're working with customers online. A lot of your success is going to come from reviews, especially if you are on Etsy or Amazon Handmade. Make sure your customers are very happy!

Happy customer checklist:

- Ship orders within a reasonable time frame, the sooner the better! Clearly state your shipping times and policies on your website so customers know what to expect. Try your best not to delay any orders. If you have a delay, make sure to let your customer know about it, and when the estimated ship date will be.
- Make sure your customers are getting automatic shipping updates, usually in the form of an email. (A lot of ecommerce platforms, like Etsy or Shopify, will do this for you.)

- Watch your shipping costs. If you are charging too much for shipping, it can really hurt your sales. Try marking up your products a little so that you can offer inexpensive or free shipping.
- Include a packing slip with your orders (this is also a good way to double-check that you're sending the right product) and add a personal "thank you for your business!" message.
- Add a little something extra with every package—such as a sticker, ribbon, or a piece of candy. You might also consider dressing up your shipping packaging. There are lots of decorative mailers you can purchase.
- Include your business card or a postcard with your social media information with orders. *Tip: I like to design thank you postcards with my branding on Vista Print, and sometimes I'll include a coupon code.*

STEP 5: MARKETING YOUR BIZ

If you're always trying to be normal, you will never know how amazing you can be.

—Maya Angelou

Social Media Advertising

Social media advertising can be tricky. Most people have a love/hate relationship with it, and it's hard to know how to use it to grow your business. If done the right way, it absolutely can help you. If done the wrong way, you can irritate and alienate your customers. Use it wisely!

Who's Following You?

You might look at a competitor's Instagram account, see that they have 11k followers, and think that means their business is doing amazing. The truth is that the number of followers or likes has nothing to do with the amount of business you are getting. It's not an accurate measure of success. The goal is to have authentic, organic, paying customers following you.

The Bandwagon

What about the (very real) perception that social media follows and likes = you are a super successful business that everyone is purchasing from? There is no doubt that, even though we can reasonably assume otherwise, our minds can jump to this conclusion. It's the bandwagon effect. It's not real. It could be that your 100 followers are actually *buying* from you, as opposed to 500 followers who have no intention of buying anything, which is often the case.

I have a friend who owns a boutique and is on Instagram. She doesn't have a huge following, but most of her followers are organic, paying customers. She says that people walk into the store asking for a product they saw on Instagram all the time. Just goes to show that you don't need a big following for social media advertising to be effective! *What matters is who is following you, not how many.*

How to Get Organic Followers

Think of who your target audience is and interact with them on social media. For example, my goal is to get my product into more gift shops and small boutiques. I look for these types of stores on Instagram and start following and liking their posts. Very often people will follow you back out of courtesy. My hope is that they will see what I make and contact me about wholesale. I even mention that I offer wholesale in my profile. It's worked several times!

Include your social media URL on all your business marketing materials — your biz card, website, and even your email signature. Ask your customers to follow you.

Remember that it takes a while to grow your tribe. Don't get frustrated. Set aside a specific block of time each day to work on social media advertising, and then walk away from it. Taking breaks is good and will help you avoid the social media time-suck trap.

Paid Social Media Advertising

Be careful and thoughtful about using paid social media advertising! You want to be sure you're gaining real customers who are interested in you and your products and not just random likes and followers from random people.

I have the perfect example of why you should be careful (learn from my mistakes, dear reader). I once had a side hustle selling my favorite essential oils. I created a Facebook page and wasn't getting a lot of traffic, so one day I pushed that ever-so-enticing "Boost Post" button to see what would happen. Much to my delight, I ended up getting around 500 likes on my page in just a few days. I was thinking to myself, "wow, that was really worth the money I paid," until over the next month it became apparent that it didn't produce any sales for me at all. ZERO. Why? I realized that most of the people who were following my page were also essential oil business owners! These followers will never convert into paying customers.

Think twice about hitting the Boost Post button, especially when you're just starting out and you have a limited marketing budget. There are lots of free things you can do to improve your following, and if you want to run a paid ad, only pay for targeted ads with specific goals in mind (read on).

Instagram—My Favorite Social Media Platform for Crafty Biz Owners

My advice for people starting out is to concentrate on one platform. Trying to manage multiple social media accounts is a lot of work. As you grow, you can expand to other platforms—and you can hire someone to help you or use a paid app that lets you pre-schedule posts. Instagram is great for arts & crafts businesses because it focuses on photos and showcasing your products. Here are some ways to start using Instagram for your biz.

Tip: Instagram is owned by Facebook. So, if you have a Facebook biz page, you can easily have your Instagram posts show up there too without a lot of extra work.

What Should You Post?

Instagram is very visual. It's all about images and photography, so it's super important that you post high-quality, beautiful, engaging images. Luckily, our modern-day smartphones all come with excellent built-in cameras, so no need to invest in expensive equipment.

Grids, Layouts, and Other Designy Things

A lot of people are now designing their Instagram feed around themes—such as a checkerboard, row by row, diagonal, or vertical line pattern. This can be really eye-catching and fun to do! It will take some pre-planning. Draw a grid in a notebook with rows of threes and write in what you plan on posting on specific days to help you achieve the look you want. Other things you can do with your photos are add borders, make them a size that's different from the standard Instagram square, or choose a unique color scheme.

Tip: you can also use a post scheduling app to help you plan out your grid, like Planoly (see Post Planners and Schedulers section).

The most important thing to do is remain consistent in your theme. You will be establishing a look and feel for your business.

#Hashtags

Hashtags are King in the Instagram world. They help people find and follow you. Make a list of hashtags in your niche. You can have as many as 30 hashtags added to your posts. Mix up the tags you are using to help you reach a new audience.

For example, if you make homemade organic goat's milk soap, you could try hashtags similar to this: #homemadesoap #goatsmilk #organicsoap #organicbathproducts. A good way to get ideas for hashtags is to look at what your competitors are using. Avoid gimmicky hashtags like #love, #likeforlike, etc. This attracts spammy comments.

To help your posts get noticed, try to find unique hashtags. To figure out how popular certain hashtags are, simply type the word you'd like to use into the search bar on Instagram. Then check the number under the hashtag. Aim for hashtags that have under 500k posts. Anything over this and your post will have too much competition to be seen.

Instagram is a visual experience. People don't like seeing your hashtags — it feels salesy. So, you need to make them less visible. You can hide them by adding space between your post text and your tags, or by making a comment on your own post with your hashtags. If you are posting a Story with hashtags, camouflage them with the same color as your background, or cover them with a sticker.

Post Planners and Schedulers

If you want the ability to pre-schedule posts on Instagram, I highly recommend using a web and mobile app scheduler.

My favorite for crafty biz girls and the one I use is called Planoly. It's specifically designed for Instagram and it's affordable. In fact, Planoly was designed by a fellow small business owner who was looking for an easier way to promote her jewelry business! Planoly lets you visually plan, manage, and schedule your Instagram posts days, weeks, or even months in advance. This can save a lot of time in the long run. I like to pre-schedule several weeks of posts at a time so I can check social media advertising off my to-do list and focus on other projects. Brilliant.

Another helpful Planoly feature — it will recommend the best times of the day to schedule your posts based on the amount of traffic your Instagram feed normally sees, so the chances of your post being seen and getting good organic reach are much greater. You can also use Planoly to schedule posts to Facebook and Twitter.

How Often Should I Post?

I get asked this question a lot, and my advice is "as many times as you think you need to in order to keep your followers interested, but not so many times that you irritate them." I aim for once a day. If it's a busy time of year, such as the holiday shopping season, I might post twice a day. If it's a less busy season, I find that every other day is enough.

Tagging Products in Your Photos / Instagram Shopping

Facebook has recently launched **Instagram Shopping**, an easy way to tag products in your photos that link to an online catalog. You can build a catalog of your products through Facebook Catalog Manager (remember that Facebook owns Instagram, so they are connected) and tag products in your catalog on your Instagram posts and Stories. This is a really easy (and free!) way for customers to purchase the products you are featuring in your posts. In order to be eligible for Instagram shopping, you will need a specific type of account, and you will need to connect your Instagram account to your catalog.

Visit the Facebook for Business website at **www.facebook.com/business** for instructions on how to set up your Instagram shopping account. You can also tag products on your Facebook business page.

When to Pay for Advertising

I have experiemented with a lot of paid advertising on Instagram, and I always get the best results when I turn an organic post into an ad. For example, if I have a post that is getting a lot of likes and comments and it has good organic reach, I will consider putting some money behind the post because I already know that people are responding well to the creative. It's a great way to test-drive your ads before you pay for them!

If you do decide to turn your post into an ad, make sure you have a specific goal in mind for your business that advertising can help to achieve. In the marketing world we call this a key performance indicator (KPI). Is your goal or KPI to see an increase of Instagram followers, or do you want increase the sales of a specific product? How much money can you afford to spend on advertising for a good return on investment (ROI)? Planning ahead and having specific goals in mind will help you make decisions that increase the likelihood of your ad being successful.

I like to schedule ads through the Instagram app. You can also schedule ads to run on Instagram through Facebook Ads Manager, but because I prefer to turn organic posts that have already been published into ads, this is best done through the Instagram app.

To get started, click on the "Promote" button beneath your post. The first screen lets you choose where to send people: Your Profile, Your Website, or Your Direct Messages. If you choose to send people to your profile, you are likely to gain Instgram followers. Sending people to your website promotes sales but less Instagram followers. The Direct Messages option will encourage people to engage in conversations with your business. Because of my business model, I almost always choose the website option and send people to a specific product on my website, because I am most interested in paying for ads that result in sales. This goal is called a conversion (another marketing term).

After selecting where to send people, you will choose your audience. This is the most important step. Always, always define your audience. Having a defined audience will help your ads reach the right people. For example, I make and sell a lot of Texas-themed products. Though I do get orders from other states (we call these "the other 49" in Texas, ha ha), the majority of purchases are made in Texas. Therefore, I'm more likely to get more sales if I only show my ads to people living in Texas. Other ways to define your audience are showing ads to people with specific interests or to specific age and gender groups. You can create and save audiences in both Instagram and Facebook Ads Manager.

How Much Should You Spend?

Another reason I like scheduling ads through the Instagram app is they do a great job of recommendng a budget that will help your ad be more effective. Watch for and follow these prompts. If you spend too little, you won't be happy with your ad performance. Instagram advertising is affordable for most small business owners. They will also recommend stretching out the number of days you are running your ad so it has the potential to reach more people.

Tip: I always see better ad results when I follow the Instagram prompts in terms of how much I want to spend per day and how long I should run my ad. They know, based on data, what will work best for your ad. And they want you to be successful so you will continue to advertise. Heed the Instagram advice prompts!

Website Landing Pages

If you decide to do website advertising, *I highly recommend that you link to a specific product page rather than to your homepage.* Don't make potential customers go looking around your website for the products they see on your Instagram posts, they will likely loose interest and you will loose the sale. You will have better results by linking your ad to a specific product page where people can easily check out and complete the sale.

Remember that when you are running an ad, you have a very small window of time *(seconds!)* to grab someone's attention and create enough interest that they will continue to interact with your content and purchase your product. You must think through every step in order to be successful. You must be posting creative, high-quality, engaging photographs or graphics, and written content that clearly explains what you are promoting and what you would like them to do next (in marketing terms this is a call to action, or CTA). Keep experimenting with your creative content. Eventually you will see a pattern and you will be able to replicate what has worked for you in the past!

Instagram Photography Tips

Instagram is a social media platform that was designed for the sharing of photographs and images. People expect to see high-quality, creative photographs in your feed! Here are a few tips on how to take your own product photos, not only for your Instagram feed, but for your product catalogs and website.
1) Take your product photos in a place with lots of soft, natural light. I like to use a wood coffee table I have in my front room that is next to a lot of floor-to-ceiling windows. Taking your photos outside is also a great idea—just don't do it in direct sunlight. Choose a nice, shady spot in afternoon light.

2) Try including props in your photos. For example, I will often photograph my tea towels on a dining room plate. Plants, flowers, and vases are always nice. Or photograph your product being used in some purposeful way.

3) Take and post authentic photos of yourself, your studio, your creative process, and your pretty face. The truth is that people are not just buying your product, they are buying YOU! Use social media to tell your story. This can be difficult if you are a shy person. For example, I really struggle with posting photos of myself—it's just not something I love to do. But when I make myself get out of my comfort zone and I post something about me or my life, it's always popular, and I know it's helping to grow my tribe. Stretch yourself a little. Help people get to know the awesome person that you are!

Photo Apps and Filters

There are a lot of great apps and filters you can use to edit your photos right on your phone. Some of my favorite apps are A Color Story for editing photos, and WordSwag for adding text to my images. I also use the built-in photo editing tools in Instagram. Do a search in the app store and see what the most popular photo and video apps currently are.

Design tip: don't alter your photo too drastically and go easy on the filters. The natural look is best.

CONGRATS, YOU'RE A BUSINESS OWNER!

Celebrate all the work you've done so far to launch your biz, hooray! You have an awesome journey ahead. You're going to have so much fun. You'll learn new things about business that you didn't know before. You will grow personally and professionally. Your products will get better and better.

What's next?...

Write a Business Plan

Now that you've started your vision board, defined your "Why," made some goals, branded your company, made financial decisions, and started a marketing strategy, you can take all this information and write a business plan. It doesn't have to be fancy! Just start with a blank sheet of paper. Cover these eight topics:

1. A one-sentence description of your biz.
2. A description of your products and how they will be made.
3. Who your target audience is.
4. Who your competition is, and what makes you different.
5. How and where you will sell your products.
6. What your projected product costs and profit margin will be.
7. How you will advertise your business.
8. What you hope to achieve in the next three months, six months, year.

If you don't feel like you have all the answers right now, it's okay! In fact, business plans are living, breathing documents that are meant to change. Think of it as a road map to achieving your goals. You might end up changing your direction, taking a new road, or heading towards a different destination than you originally planned. It's about the journey! Taking the time to write a business plan will be a helpful exercise in making the transition from hobby to business owner.

What to Do When You Get Stuck

Sometimes you'll be movin' and groovin' and things are going well, and then you'll hit a wall. Don't worry! This is a good time to take a look at what is working and what is not in your biz. Here are a few ideas to get the wheels rolling again.

Spend time with a good friend and bounce around ideas or get feedback. One of my best-selling products started out as a suggestion from a friend. Getting another viewpoint can be really helpful and get you moving again.

Make a list of what has and hasn't been working in your biz. Look at your sales. Which products are selling best? Go through your Instagram or social media feed and look at which posts are getting the most likes and comments. You may see a pattern. Maybe one of your products is getting more attention than others. If so, expand on that idea and see if you can come up with some new product ideas in a similar vein.

If you need to grow your tribe, brainstorm new ways of advertising. Maybe you could cross-promote your products with another business owner. Or you could donate product to a raffle or fundraiser that fits your target audience. Try participating in a vendor event to meet new people. Or start a blog about your product and creative process.

Sometimes it helps to take a break for a while (but set a date for when you're coming back). I always feel more creative after a vacation, or even taking a day off gives me enough time to clear my head. Being creative takes a lot of energy, so make sure you aren't getting burned out. When you're feeling refreshed and ready to work again, you may see some things about your biz that you didn't see before. Hitting your creative restart button is always a good idea!

Keep Going, Girl!

Remember that it takes most people a lot of work to build a successful business. It's easy to look at your competitors and think they were an overnight success, but in truth most of them have worked very hard for a long time to get to where they are.

Your business is like a flower. Start by planting a seed, give it the care it needs, and then after a lot of consistent work, you will see it bloom. It's going to be beautiful!

A Few Words of Advice from Crafty Biz Owners Like You

One of the things I love most about being a small business owner is the camaraderie I feel with others who are aspiring to the same goals I am. We can easily appreciate and understand the effort that goes into trying to build a creative business around our craft, and I have made a lot of wonderful friends along the way. I asked a few of them what their best tips would be for someone just getting started, and their answers are below!

"You are going to fail and that's okay. The important part is to get up, dust yourself off and try a new approach."

"Don't try to please everybody. Go in the direction that best suits your business and your life."

"Do the scary things and let it change you!"

"Ask your friends what they like to buy and what they would pay for your items. Participate in vendor events to see if there is a market for your product. This is the best kind of research."

"Don't be shy about marketing your product. Be diligent in your social media and marketing campaigns to grow your tribe. Really put yourself out there and be your authentic self."

"Make weekly and monthly goals. It will keep you in check and help your business grow."

"Just do it! Regardless of the outcome, you will learn so many new things and grow from your experiences."

"Network with other arts & crafts business owners. Ask them what is working and not working for their business, and if they have advice on other vendor shows that are working best for them, retailers that may be interested in your products, etc. The more connections you make the more successful you will be."

Business Launch CHECKLIST

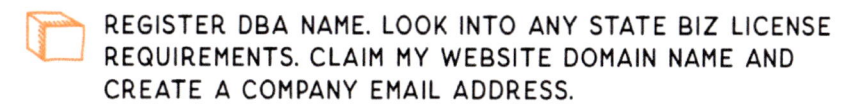

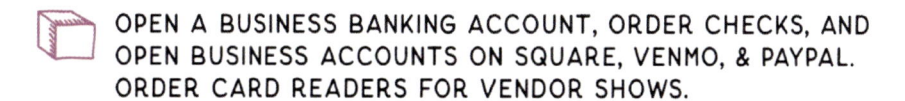

LAUNCH DATE:

- ☐ REGISTER DBA NAME. LOOK INTO ANY STATE BIZ LICENSE REQUIREMENTS. CLAIM MY WEBSITE DOMAIN NAME AND CREATE A COMPANY EMAIL ADDRESS.

- ☐ OPEN A BUSINESS BANKING ACCOUNT, ORDER CHECKS, AND OPEN BUSINESS ACCOUNTS ON SQUARE, VENMO, & PAYPAL. ORDER CARD READERS FOR VENDOR SHOWS.

- ☐ BRANDING: GET COMPANY LOGO DESIGNED & BUSINESS CARDS MADE. MAKE A STYLE GUIDE FOR ADVERTISING. CREATE A VISION BOARD FOR MY BIZ LOOK & FEEL.

- ☐ PRODUCTS: MAKE A LIST OF ALL SUPPLIES USED IN THE MAKING OF MY PRODUCT AND WHERE THEY WILL BE PURCHASED. RESEARCH PRODUCTION PARTNERS.

- ☐ PRODUCT PACKAGING: DESIGN PACKAGING SOLUTION FOR BOTH ONLINE & RETAIL.

- ☐ PURCHASE ANY NEEDED SHIPPING SUPPLIES, MAILERS, BOXES, BUBBLE WRAP, TAPE, ETC.

- ☐ MAKE A PRICING LIST FOR WHOLESALE AND RETAIL. CALCULATE PROFIT MARGINS.

- ☐ DESIGN VENDOR BOOTH. GET SIGNAGE MADE. PURCHASE TENT, TABLES, AND DISPLAY FIXTURES.

- ☐ WORK ON MARKETING STRAGEGY. SET UP SOCIAL MEDIA ACCOUNTS, EMAIL NEWSLETTER, ETC.

- ☐ DECIDE ON ECOMMERCE PLATFORM AND BUILD ONLINE STORE (ETSY, SHOPIFY, ETC.)

- ☐ WRITE BUSINESS PLAN FOR THE YEAR. CELEBRATE THE LAUNCH OF MY BUSINESS!

follow me
@SPICEWOODANDROSE

I would love to have you follow me on social media and tell me how your biz is going!

Follow Spicewood & Rose on Instagram
@spicewoodandrose
or Facebook at
www.facebook.com/spicewoodandrose

You can find my crafty biz shop at
www.spicewoodandrose.com
or **Etsy.com/SpicewoodAndRose**

Made in the USA
Columbia, SC
06 February 2021